Glimpses of Life

The Commuters Companion

I0117841

Georgina Wakefield

chipmunkapublishing
the mental health publisher

Published by
Chipmunkapublishing
PO Box 6872
Brentwood
Essex CM13 1ZT
United Kingdom

http://www.chipmunkapublishing.com

Chipmunkapublishing gratefully acknowledge the support of Arts Council England.

Author Biography

I wrote this book immediately after completing my first book 'Schizophrenia A Mother's Story' which charts my youngest sons 19 year battle with Paranoid Schizophrenia his journey began when he was 16 years old or thereabouts. The book charts the journey that his family was forced to take in order to support him. Writing about our experiences was extremely cathartic and it's helped me no end.

Almost two decades on Christian now has a far better quality of life. He lives independently, works part time and he also employs a Personal Assistant through the Government Direct Payment scheme. Following 7 very difficult years Christian relapsed at the age of 23 he was admitted to hospital. I went out shopping for some toiletries for him. I was feeling dreadful and when I parked the car I took up 2 spaces because I couldn't think straight. A young man started shouting at me, he was telling me how useless I was and that I shouldn't be allowed to drive a car. He became extremely abusive [even though there were plenty of other parking spaces]. I can remember thinking if only you knew how I feel and what is going on in my life at the moment. This book hopefully highlights the fact that life can be very hard for us sometimes. For the past 10 years I have worked in Mental Health providing presentations to Professionals which I believe helps to deepen their understanding of 'The Carer's Perspective'. I use poetry from my books simply because poetry condenses what were saying and makes it far more powerful. I soon realized that by using poetry I could tell the story in a fraction of the time that it would take to explain in text. Due to the pace of life these days we never seem to have the time to read books this one could be read on a train journey. The book consists of 61 short stories about the continual ups and downs of life. I decided to write 61 because I am 61 and hopefully I have learned things about life as it's gone on. Life as we all know can be funny but it can also be very sad the book is about many problems that we human beings have to deal with some of which you yourself will have come across. Those of you with a good memory will recognize characters from previous stories as your reading the book.

'Glimpses Of Life' is mainly fictional but some parts are based on fact for instance my Sisters story 'Side By Side' also some of my own experiences pop up now and then. People who know me will possibly recognize themselves occasionally too you have been warned.

My Sister sadly lost her fight for life on December 4th 2009 I am currently writing a book entitled Anyone Who Had A Heart which includes some of her experiences in various hospitals . Chipmunka Publishing have agreed to publish the book hopefully later this year.

'Glimpses of Life'

Have you ever stood in a Supermarket queue bored to death? What a silly question of course you have, one day I was extremely bored, I started to people watch thinking I wonder what he does for a living? I wonder where they like to eat out? Have they got kids? Are they happy together? Do they wish they could break away from each other? God I thought we are all so very different   people can be pleasant but some are unpleasant, some are cheerful others are miserable some are optimist's some are pessimists. Some have a good marriage others? Disastrous. Some people do really meaningful jobs others very boring and on top of that we all differ in our opinions on so many things. We also have to deal with so many different situations some good some bad some have probably been through really traumatic experiences bereavement, divorce whilst others remain virtually untouched by life's hardships and tragedies. As I studied them I began to make up fictional stories about them and this book is the end result.

Glimpses of Life

Front cover designed by Denise Claxton

Georgina Wakefield

Glimpses of Life

They push their wire trolleys around the many aisles
Some are looking miserable others spare a smile
Bread tea sugar cans of beans cola peas and cakes
Biscuits butter cheese and jam sweets and frosted flakes
Some look very prosperous others look quite poor
Some look full of fun others quite a bore
Some have happy carefree lives for others life is tough
Some look kind and gentle others look quite rough
There's a lady in a smart blue suit blue bag blue shoes blue hair
Her hubby looks quite hen pecked but who said life was fair?
There's a young man buying hair gel wrigleys, deoderant whisky
Perhaps he's got a red hot date and he's feeling rather frisky
A young woman in aisle 5 has a very sad look in her eyes
A man whose hooked on crack cocaine is bent on getting high
You may recognise a mother a husband or a wife
Join me at the checkout queue to take a glimpse of life

The Eternal Optimist

No one ever said life was easy

In the endless shopping queue I visualise
their lives

The lady on checkout 6 is finding it hard to survive

Her clothes are very well worn well worn shoes are from
Oxfam she's wearing

She buys penny saver brands and under her breath she keeps
swearing

She hauls it all home on the bus with 2 screaming kids in tow

Her appearance reflects her poverty keep out of those bags
Danny no!!!

She's relieved that he won't be home this week he's working
on lates

The kids start to fight yet again as she empties some chips on
their plates

Sometimes she gets a beating she begins to despise him a lot

But there's nowhere to go if she leaves so she settles for what
she's got

The beatings are getting more frequent made worse by his trips
the pub

Or if she fakes a headache, sometimes it's over his grub

They don't seem to know each other discussions are rarely

heard

She dreams of a life without him as happy and as free as a bird

He keeps her short of money he's selfish through and through

As for knowing the cost of living he hasn't got a clue
He knows how much a pint costs he's very generous to his mates

They think he's a diamond geezer when it's his round nobody waits

She much prefers the winter she can wear her wrap around cape

The cape has enormous pockets decked with pieces of sticky tape

But she's not one of those weirdoes's who enjoy the buzz stealing brings

It's more a need for survival she desperately needs the things

She clocks the Security Guard he's gassing with his mate

Will she feel his hand on her shoulder? She gets in a terrible state

She uses the kids as lookouts they think its all part of a game
She does this purely for them so the need overpowers the shame

She did try to leave him once they ended up in a halfway home

The kids nearly drove her insane she felt even more alone

Money was even tighter she was forced to sell the TV

In the end the poverty won proved harder than being free

She dreaded going back to him but she really couldn't cope

So she pulled on all her resources and held on to fragile hope

She hated him with a vengeance she felt soul- less and dreadfully weak

Stupid bitch I'm pathetic as for him he's just a control freak

He helped her with the move borrowed his brothers old van

He chucked the lot in the back she thought to herself 'lovely man!!!!!!

She'd packed in black plastic sacks she could never afford suitcases

Told herself this is for my kids just look at their happy faces

She decided to keep her mouth shut she was far too weary to fight

He thought she deserved a lesson so she got a sound beating that night

She drags a comb through her hair the roots are through half a mile

The blonde ends are broken and brittle she really needs a restyle

Glimpses of Life

She knows it will have to wait besides no one looks at her
locks
The kids are in desperate need of new underwear and new
socks!!!!!!

Her mind wanders back to him did she love him way back in
the past?

But she doesn't do self pity her mind feels more settled at last

She'd love to be treated with kindness she longs to be
tenderly kissed

But it's doubtful that either will happen to the Eternal
Optimist

The Sadness of Old Age

It comes to us all

The elderly lady on 3 has just had a hip operation

She wishes she hadn't bothered she keeps getting a clicking sensation

There's a dispute going on between her and a kindly sales assistant

She keeps trying to help her pack her bags but the old lady remains insistent

I've been packing my own bags for years dear I know you're just being kind

But I've no one to help me at home so I'll manage if you don't mind!!!

Her gaze falls on the couple on 2 her eyes mist with unshed tears

He's holding a tiny white bundle her mind wanders back through the years

Can it be half a century ago? They were blissfully happy like them

Blonde headed dimpled babies treasured by her and Len

Once the kids left home a divorce seemed to be the best way

They didn't have much left in common Len bored her to death anyway

Glimpses of Life

He had a peculiar hobby he liked to measure rainfall

She didn't share his interest she couldn't understand him at all

He never said you look great dear she'd long for him to be nice

They tried a marriage counsellor but he didn't take her advice

Len was the biggest fool he didn't even try she lost count of the times of the times

She'd screamed Jesus Christ Len you don't even try!!!

I'm a mans man he'd often say I'm not into niceties

She wasn't asking for much she wasn't hard to please

Are you ok there dear? the checkout girl's voice brings her back

Sorry dear I'm miles away I'll get a spurt on to pack

She can see the couple on 2 are mesmerised can life ever get better than this?

She smiles at the love on their faces mumbling 'those days were sheer bliss'

She wonders how long she's got left as she ponders on life and death

Jesus my hip is so painful she stops to catch up on her breath

Sometimes she thinks what's the point? Will we when we reach this stage?

Take heed it comes to us all 'The Sadness Of Old Age.!!!!!

Such A Conniving Pair

A reflection of life [for some people] in 2010

The old ladies blonde dimpled babies have comfortable lives of their own

They are concerned about mother she'd be far better off in a home!!!!!!

David's a brilliant lawyer and visits at least once a year

You can't keep being so stubborn Mother do I make myself crystal clear?

Don't adopt that tone with me son your not in your courtroom now

I won't give up my house!!! Christ almighty the stubborn old cow!!!!

Daughter Jane climbs the social ladder she's more interested in wealth

Hubby works in the Stock Exchange and it doesn't do much for his health

He'll probably die from a heart attack possibly before he's 40

Their kids go to a private school obnoxious, greedy, and haughty

They have many expensive holidays in 5 star hotels abroad

They complain about almost everything and are either fighting or bored

They have every conceivable luxury clothes with designer labels

They both attend a private school it's a fortune a term at Green Gables

The grand children refuse to stay over they prefer to stay at home

They never think of what Gran wants or the time she spends on her own
Jane's much the same as David but she's not nearly quite so kind

She speaks to her Mother harshly she's not scared to speak her mind

The house just isn't clean Mother Christ the smell of that mangy old dog

She sprays her expensive perfume if she's forced to use the bog

Jane I've got an idea luvvie what if we come to live with you?

I'd have to bring my commode and old Bobby will have to come too

Oh sorry dear I forgot you've only got 4 bedrooms free

There just wouldn't be enough room for my dog my commode and me

 Please try not to worry about me dear I know your just being kind
But I brought you both up in this house so I'll die here if you don't mind!!!!!!

Glimpses of Life

She's definitely losing her marbles she thinks as she walks down the hall

 I really can't cope with much more she's driving me clean up the wall !!!!!!

I've got a really good friend a Doctor said David he'll sort this out for a tidy price

We can sign all the relevant papers and he'll give us some sound advice

I'll give him a bell tomorrow it'll cost us both a few thou

Worth it for peace of mind though I'm drawing my share out right now

This old place can go up for sale we'll split the money 2 ways

We can burn her old rubbish after sorting it out most of it's seen better days
Do you want to keep these old photo's Jane there's one here of you me and Mum?

No said Jane my life's moved on and this place is like a slum

You sound a bit like a snob Jane David quipped with a wry grin

I'd hate my friends to see them she said as she chucks them all in the bin

What about the bloody mutt though? Lets face it it's seen better days

My cleaner will take him to be put down that's the kindest

way

God the smell of the bloody thing it stinks the whole place out

We'll have it fumigated clear all of rubbish right out

Have you checked her bank accounts? you can bet there's a tidy pile

You'll be pleasantly surprised Jane replied
flashing David a smile

Christ I almost forgot she's uses a post office book

It's in that writing desk we may as well take a look

Our minds will feel more settled soon we can visit and check how she's been

I can't wait to get this sorted we make quite a clever team

 She warms her hands by the fire blissfully unaware

That her blonde dimpled blue eyed babies are 'Such A Conniving Pair'.

Like A Tiger In A Cage

Loneliness is like a disease

The old lady and husband Len parted some years before

Len's never really understood why she found him such a bore

Lots of people like collecting, coins, butterflies, stamps and old books

Len had no interest in how she felt what she wore or how she looked

The kids don't bother to visit Len they blame him for the break

They have to visit their Mother though both being on the make

Len moved into sheltered housing with a buzzer on 24 call

A Matron with low level patience they drive her right up the wall

His hobby is to stand at the window watching the world passing by

He often feels very lonely and more often has a good cry

He knows that today must be Tuesday when he sees the Laundry Van

He shouts out cup of char Jack best china teapot in hand

Jack quickly checks his watch ok Len but make it quick

He mutters under his breath Jesus Christ Len gets on my wick

Always gawking out of the window nothing bloody better to do

He never stops to consider his life will get just like that too

He swigs it down in an instant needs must when the devil drives

You can't do enough for a good guvner mate and I ain't one o them that skives

Still tomorrows Wednesday they play Bingo in the big hall

Takes up well over an hour it might even be his turn to call

2 fat ladies 88 that gives em all a good laugh

Then if the waters warm enough a nice hot soak in the bath

66 clickerty click legs 11 gone to heaven

He'll joke with Maud and he'll argue with John

There's always something going on

He ponders on the years gone by when the kids were young
Sometimes he forgets he's got a Daughter and a Son

He's still unable to see where he went so wrong

She was far too demanding an ungrateful bitch all along

He paces and pads up and down like a Tiger in a cage

Then he stops and stares out of the window

What's Mum Cooked For Dinner?

Teenagers, can you remember that very first date? Sheer terror that something will go terribly wrong, these 3 teenagers will never forget theirs

A slip of a girl on 9 is worried about her skin

In her basket facial potions that'll probably end up in the bin

She thinks her bum is enormous she'd die to be thinner than this

Will he notice the fat and the acne as they tenderly share their first kiss

At the thought she freezes with fear he's gorgeous and his skin is soooo good

She's waited so long for this date so the fear overrides the mood

She imagines him fumbling around clumsily undoing her bra

She's frantic what will she do? Hadn't planned on things going this far

Say he feels my rolls of fat and mistakes em for my tits?

She can almost hear him laughing rolling around in fits

What if he wants a blowjob? And my bloody teeth get in the way?

Her best mate did a demo they couldn't stop laughing that day

She asked her how she should hold it loosely? Or should it be

21

tight?

They invested in half a cucumber to use as a prototype

After lots of mucking around she gave it up as a very bad job

She'll just have to give it a shake besides who wants one of them in their gob?

They decided they should provide lessons Christ they cater for everything else

You could learn how to suck and when to blow and not make a fool of yourself .

They could even give out diplomas to the ones that can do it the best

They'd learn not to go at it hammer and tongs you know take time out to rest

She worries about almost everything foreplay and the art of French kissing

Her mate said when she gets the hang of it she'll soon see what she's been missing

He reminds her of Leonardo De Caprio his blue eyes simply curl up her toes

She prays God will do her a favour and produce a boil on his nose
Then she wouldn't look so ugly she can't possibly cancel this date

Perhaps a huge zit would suffice how on earth did she get in this state?

She'd love to look like Maddona and share just a few of her charms

Bet her tits stay up when she's flat on her back whereas mine end up under her arms

In the end she blames her Mother it's her fault that she's not thinner

Jesus that's never the time I wonder 'What Mum's Cooked For My Dinner?

A Risky Business

Thank god he didn't see her he was right at the back of the queue

Stocking up on his hair gel stuff to spray down his trousers too

She'd be totally mortified if she'd turned round to find

 That Leo was right there behind her just say he can read her mind!!!!!!!!

But he's in a stupor too can't stop thinking about tonight

Will she tingle with unleashed passion? Will everything go alright?
He'll tell he's had lots of experience he's had sex loads of times now

What goes on under his bedclothes is his business anyhow

But what if it goes all floppy? He'll invest in a bottle of scotch

Some wrigleys to drown out the smell but then say it won't go up a notch?

Best to start as he means to go on he wasn't going to come [pardon the pun]

He'd be clutching a box of Lemsip and tell her he's rowed with his Mum

He feels sure it's a better idea to fake the flu from the start

He'd die on the spot at the prospect of one of them dropping a fart

Glimpses of Life

By the time he reaches the checkout she'd disappeared on the bus

The girl on the till eyes him up he must stop making a fuss

He blames Brad from 4B for his terror Brads first time didn't go well
Brads petrified to try it again in fact it was bloody hell

Why had she started to laugh? Why couldn't she share the joke?

He knows it's a funny shape but she'd put him right off his stroke

It's rather like a banana he dreams of an op one day

Would they be able to straighten it? And how much would he have to pay?

His mum says he's making too much fuss she just treats it all as a joke

To him the problems enormous it puts him clean off his stroke

She even told his aunt Betty they were giggling at his plight

What if she tells all of the family knowing her she might
Brads decided to wait till he's older it's far safer to rely on his hand

He'll try to get that op but will the GP understand?

So he made up his mind once and for all he'd have to rely on he's luck

He'd pray things wouldn't go pear shaped it's such a risk with your very first f…!!!

The Girl on Checkout 9

She's always wanted to be a nurse

The girl working on checkout 9 spies a boy at the back of her queue

He reminds her of Leonado De Caprio and she's never seen eyes that blue

Should she dare to ask for a date? The very thought makes her fingers shake

She's never done it before it's a risk that she's longing to take

He throws his stuff on the belt hair gel deodorant whisky

He smiles and gives her a wink, bet he can be very frisky

Courage wells up inside of her but her voice comes out shaky and thin

You'll be needing some Alka Seltzers he flashes her a grin
Why don't you be my nurse? Christ she thinks luck at last

I must think of something witty and I'll have to think of it fast

I'll need to go home for my uniform I finish at 8 tonight

Don't forget your fishnets that would be quite a sight

I'm only pulling your leg oh don't be so boring she said

Jesus I've gone up to heaven I can't wait to get this one to bed

She's obviously really experienced ok 8 o'clock he says fine

SHE TINGLES WITH EXCITEMENT the girl on checkout 9

If only he knew her secret there's only been the one time with
that Brad
She cringes at Brad's embarrassment it was really ever so sad

She peeked when he took his pants off it was such a hilarious
sight

Shaped just like a banana so she told him to turn off the light

But she couldn't contain her amusement at seeing his bent
banana

It all bubbled up to the surface then she erupted in raucous
laughter

Poor brad went extremely red she'll feel guilty forevermore

She'd dressed at incredible speed she couldn't wait to get out
of the door

But she's convinced tonight will be different everything is
bound to go fine

She tingles at the very thought the girl on checkout 9

Blue Rinse

'We've all met this lady she's had a trouble free life and she wouldn't cope well at all with her hubby's dark secret.

The lady on checkout 0 looks around 55

Her bags are filled with the dearest brands she's so happy to be alive

Hubby John's always had a good job retires soon on a very good pension

One day they'll enjoy his retirement with too many vacations to mention

She dreams of those golden days John's just bought her a brand new Ford

It didn't dent their bank account it was easy for them to afford

Both kids are studying at UNI their lives are so comfy and neat

A bungalow that people would die for in a very respectable street

They've just bought a new conservatory it's enormous and so well equipped

Comes to twenty thou the salesman said that's fine Blue Rinse had quipped

Her wardrobes are full to bursting enough clothes to start a shop

John gave up many moons ago he knows she'll never stop

As long as it keeps her happy that's just Johns view on life

He knows there's no point arguing besides she's a dutiful wife

She's just had her hair tinted blue again to match her smart new suit

She tells John to push her trolley but be careful dear don't scratch the boot
John's bought her a matching wardrobe new shoes scarves, handbags too

Next week their off on a cruise they so love the QE 2

They'll dine at the Captains table and pile on a stone for sure

They must remember to pack the new camera John forgot it the year before

She'll drive him mad with her flashing show the neighbours when they get back

He'll moan at her what's your hurry she's off round there before they unpack

It gives the neighbours a laugh though when they return from one of stints

Behind her back they all snigger together just look who's coming Blue Rinse!!!!!!

Only Now And Again

Poor John

Blue rinses hubby John has a problem but she doesn't know

When she goes off to her Bridge Club John dresses up in her clothes

It makes him feel so much better in a strange way it makes him feel calm

He knows his wife would be horrified but it doesn't do any harm

He was forced to confide in a neighbour number 15 name of Rose

She came round to borrow some milk and caught him painting his toes

She was very understanding though, she said John just forget the milk

I've a blouse indoors just your colour bright red and made of pure silk

He finds it such a comfort how well Rose can understand

She often lends him her lipstick and more often takes hold of his hand

Takes all types to make a world John well that's my philosophy

We can't possibly be all the same dear what kind of world would it be?

His dream is to go out as a woman Rose builds on his confidence

If you think it would make you feel better dear then to me it makes perfect sense

At last he finds the courage but standing on Tower Hill Station

He was seen by of one of his workmates Brian who brags he's a Mason

John froze to the spot mortified couldn't think of what he should do

In a fit of blind panic he hitched up his skirt and ran into the ladies loo

His hand shook repairing his lipstick seconds felt much more like hours

A lady washing her hands said oooh what a lovely blouse!!!

He tried hard to sound like a woman but things didn't go quite to plan

The lady threw up her arms screaming loudly Christ it's a man!!

The upshot of poor John's adventure was he ended up in the cells

It attracted a very big crowd most of London heard his yells

Blue rinse was saved from it all and John managed to wriggle out

Glimpses of Life

When he and Rose talk of his nightmare they end up falling about

But what if Blue Rinse had found out? He wouldn't be living in clover

Christ she'd never forgive me Rose my marriage would have been over

There's plenty more fish in the sea John, Rose gently takes hold of his hand

She'd be there waiting to claim him all part of a far bigger plan

Things moved on with their friendship their feelings got out of control

Blue Rinse is totally in the dark about Rose filling the mistress's role

John's tried so many times to stop but life becomes too much of a strain

Besides he can use 2 wardrobes now and it's only now and again

Playing The Game

The next 4 are all in their thirties and although they can't see it they are all heading for big trouble meet wife Angie, husband Barry, Susie the secretary and Jack the milkman

The thirty-something's on 5 are all looking a little bit fraught

Their marriage's have hit a bad patch Barry's frightened of getting caught

If she'd showed him a bit more affection he'd never have gone astray

What she doesn't know won't hurt her she's frigid anyway!!!!

He reflects on when things were so different before the brats came along

But now things have changed so much he's asks himself-where *she* went wrong

There were times when sex was frantic as if it might go out of fashion

Her story? He's never romantic and that's why it's lost it's passion

Last week he had a brain wave I'm going swimming he said

In the garage he left a bucket of bleach Ange was already in bed

He dipped his trunks in wrung them out he wrapped them up in a towel

He went in ready for a row wearing an angry scowl

You stink of chloride she winged as he gingerly climbed into
bed

They put too much in the water these days I've got a terrible
head

But last night was a close shave when he told her I'm out for a
jog
Then froze in disbelief when Angie said ok take the dog

He could only stay for half an hour the bloody thing whined at
the door

Susie kept on complaining what the hell did you bring that
mutt for?!!!!!!

They made do with a knee trembler didn't make it to the bed

Jesus Christ are you off already Bas? Then silence no more to
be said

Christ he thinks she's a moaner, I really do put myself out

I must always remember my condoms I'd hate to get her up
the spout

Ok she does look fantastic but Ange doesn't nag me a lot

I know how much my Angie loves me she's grateful for what
she's got
Besides she's a fabulous cook her cooking would be hard to
beat

Susie's far better in the sack but she's not really up my street

She's more interested in pedicures, beauty parlours are just
the ticket

But give her a brillo pad and she'd tell you where you can stick it

She just not into marigolds it's just not my forte says Sue

Hoovers, dusters are not her scene nor is putting her hand down the loo

Angie reaches into her trolley she smiles thinking of the next day

The milkman collects on Fridays and they always have it away

He winks and says I've got your gold top will madam be wanting cream?
He comes from the council estate good looking and quite a scream

The milkman is so romantic and he often brings a red rose

His kisses are so amazing the very thought of him curls up her toes

For the rest of the day she's in heaven he makes her feel so good

She hums as she's cooking the tea Bas thinks Christ she's in a good mood

Have you had a good day at the office Bas? The usual crap quite a bore

Susie helped me with my bloody filing [they'd had it away on the floor]

She's aware Bas is not there beside her then she sees him

Glimpses of Life

coming and glowers

His hands are behind his back I went back love to buy you
these flowers!!!!
The gesture makes her feel guilty Bas feels exactly the same

He takes hold of her hand she allows it
Then they go back to Playing The Game

One Day

Is there anymore gull able than a woman in love?!!!! I doubt it meet Susie Barry's secretary

One day the secretary thinks I just know he'll leave her one day

Good morning dear I'm leaving yes I know it's been 15 years

Pack my things while I'm at the office and there's no need for all of those tears

He says this when Susie nags him oh why can't she understand?

She whispers I'm sorry I'll wait dear then she gently strokes his hand

She knows that he stays for the children it's not that easy to leave

Better when their a bit older if he left them now they would grieve
He tells her that Angie is frigid for a year it's been separate beds

That's miles away from the truth but she swallows the lies that she's fed

Susie imagines Angie - really ugly and far too plump

But if she questions him on Angie's looks it always gives him the hump

What they have together is special he tells her this all of the time

Glimpses of Life

She knows the wait will be worth it one day he'll be mine all
mine!!!!!!

He's not stupid he knows what he's getting she almost lives at
the gym

Likes to keep herself firm and supple likes to look her best
just for him

Leg waxing every week her shapely legs look so nice
False nails by a top manicurist worth it at double the price

She's well known at the tanning parlour her body looks great
with a tan

There are no lengths she wouldn't go to satisfy her man

She's been saving for years for an uplift her breasts are
important to him

The money the pain just don't matter she thinks to herself with
a grin

Angie's the biggest fool though she should look after her
looks

Instead of Tupperware parties she should invest in some good
beauty books

No wonder he doesn't sleep with her besides he knows what
he's got

Every male in the office would love to be him they all think
she's hot hot hot
He says Angie did look good once before the kids came along

But she's let herself go in a big way he'd get more pleasure from mowing the lawn

But Angie is always complaining that bloody thing never lays down

But if she fakes a headache he walks round the house with a frown

She swears that thing will stay erect even after your dead

They'll drill a hole in your coffin Bas she told him this morning in bed

It's just like a bloody tent pole Bas it's sticking right in my back

He thinks of Susie and consoles himself at least she's good in the sack!!!!!!

He finds it so hard to get out though [bless him]
Pretends that he loves to jog last night would you believe it?

He turned up soaked with the dog

All this just for me she thought poor baby he loves me so much

How can she be so gull able so amazingly out of touch!!!!!!

The bloody mutt whined at the door for the whole of the time he was there

She'd really made an effort too with her Ann Summers underwear

She felt a little abused when he left after half an hour

She'd planned on quite a session ending up with them sharing a shower

When he'd gone she felt quite guilty poor Barry he does what he can

I must try to be more understanding he's such a lovely man

He clearly loved her to make such an effort she's sure of his love anyway

She just knows it will be before Christmas the secretary thinks One Day!!!!!!!

Collars and leads

Jack the lad the milkman

Jack dons a huge gold medallion an open necked shirt shows his hairs
Wife Beryl is well in the dark but Jack's had his share of affairs

The lady at 24 Boscome has just given birth to his child

Beryl closely resembles a field mouse small and meek and mild

His child will be kept a secret her old man thinks it's his

Jack hasn't shown much interest he thinks he's really the biz

They reside in a house full of poodles she likes to take them to shows

He encourages her in her hobby when she's gone he's off on his toes

She treats all 7 like babies her beautiful darling girls

She's been on a course for grooming she's forever tending their curls

Some have even won trophies she polishes them till they shine

She's even bought a display shelf he calls it her f….g. shrine

The milkman's obsessed with his looks well aware he's a handsome man

Glimpses of Life

Detests those strands of grey he pulls them out whenever he can

She won't leave her babies in kennels she's worried they'll catch kennel cough

The more she dotes on her babies the more he likes having it off

He consoles himself with his ladies they supply the attention he needs

Her life is ruled by her furry friends his life is sowing his seeds

He secretly detests her babies the house always swimming in puddles

But her babies supply her affection she's forever giving them cuddles

Not much goes on in their bedroom he's always too tired poor man

Beryl never complains though she tells him Jack I understand

So they carry on with their lives different things fulfil both their needs

He'll never need Viagra and she can poke her Collars And Leads

Wouldn't It Be A Sin?

This one is personal to me, this man actually exists and he felt it was more important not to change the look of a Street than consider people who are struggling with a mental illness..

The Councillor on checkout 10 feels rather irate somehow

He's opposing a housing project and he needs some answers right now

Their turning a house into flats but he doesn't like the idea

It will take away the character but what character isn't quite clear

The purpose of the project is for people who aren't quite right

They suffer from mental illnesses and should really be kept out of sight

He's not really bothered about them, their of no importance to him

But he won't let them change the look of that Street that's nothing short of a sin

He checks his watch in annoyance can't make his Committee wait

They'll desperately need his input and he can't afford to be late

He thinks life would stop without him his input is needed for sure

Glimpses of Life

His colleagues truly detest him he's a fat irritating old bore

He's full of piss and importance they say
he's so full of himself the prat

But he remains undeterred he's the bollocks and that is that

Hurry things up young lady I can't possibly be late for my meeting
My people rely on my input and there'll be problems with the seating

The Councillor should watch his blood pressure even though it's important to him

Or he could end up having a heart attack and Wouldn't That Be A Sin?

Beaten and Ravaged By Life

Meet Derek he's a Security Guard and life hasn't been very kind to him

The middle aged man on 7 looks beaten and ravaged by life

He lives in a tiny bed sit and he's lonely without the wife

She left him the summer before last just ran off one day with his mate

He'd love to strangle the pair of them his eyes narrow reflecting his fate

He throws down his bits from the basket onto the moving belt

The bastards should pay for there actions they'll never know how he felt

4 frozen dinners for one 6 eggs some milk and some tea

2 thick cut loaves of bread buy one and get one free

He chucks down a £20 note runs his hands through his thinning grey hair

I've forgotten the washing powder to hell with it what do I care?

She stitched him up good and proper got the house and he got the car

She told him lets face it your useless it was all out bloody war

In his bed sit he watches the telly and rests in an overstuffed seat

Glimpses of Life

The room is drab and smelly due to his sweaty feet

The pillows are old and stained he could do with some pillow cases

He passes wind rather loudly as he bends down to tie up his laces
At least I can't hear her nagging I can fart whenever I like

She was frigid anyway I swear that bitch was a dike

Always making excuses headaches, backaches galore

He got to rely on his hand just to remember what it was for

Sod the expense he curses I could murder a pint of cold beer

I'll give Fred a game of dominoes his old ladies left him I hear

Fred says he's over the moon though he just can't believe his luck

Cheer up Del look at me I don't give a flying f..k

No more misery and moaning I'd much rather pay for a shag
When it's over I'm so contented then I really enjoy a fag

But Derek still feels bitter thought he'd end his days with a wife

Which short of a miracles unlikely he's been Beaten And Ravaged By Life

Georgina Wakefield

Rocking in the Aisle

Her new man is not quite as nice as he seems

Derek's ex wife Tracey sees him standing there at the till

She scoots down the cereal aisle the very sight of him makes
her feel ill

She left him for someone much better has his own business in
town

He washes out the wheelie bins and wears a permanent frown

He's buying her council house they have Chinese food once a
week

Go to Garden Centres on Sundays then home to a good cut of
meat

Tracey loves the Mecca Bingo he stays at home with the girls

The oldest is nearly 15 and he loves her golden curls

She walks through the house in her undies her body
voluptuous and firm

But lately she's felt him staring the thought of it makes her
squirm

His eyes bore through her like lasers thank God she can't hear
what he's thinking

Her skin creeps when he stares like a rattle snake rarely
blinking

One night he'll take his chances who knows how this could

Glimpses of Life

turn out

He'd have to be careful though mustn't get her up the spout

She was right to leave beaten and ravaged such ambition
Security guard!!!!

The wheelie bin man's a good man and her life isn't nearly as
hard
There's nothing he wouldn't do he runs them around in his
van

He teaches the girls so much he's a truly wonderful man

He's teaching the oldest one archery she can feel his breath on
her cheek

He wraps his arms right around her she feels too nervous to
speak

Back in the cereal aisle they both give a smirk and a smile

Wheelie man and Dereks old lady end up Rocking In The
Aisle.

A Normal Home

Teenage pregnancy what a waste of youth

The young lady on checkout 12 is getting bigger each day

How will she ever conceal it? She really must find a way

If only she didn't feel sick she pretends it's a tummy bug

Her Mum keeps giving her funny looks God she could do with a hug

She begged him to leave her alone but he kept coming into her room

Now she can feel it kicking an impostor in her womb

Why did she keep going to bingo? What on earth will she do when she knows?

How can she stop it from happening every day she can feel it grow

What made him pick on her? He meets women he washes their bins

Now her life's ruined forever will God pay him back for his sins?

What if Mum doesn't believe her? Will she think that she led him on?

How she wishes her Mum hadn't met him how she wishes that he were gone

Should she confide in her father? Would he believe her

although it's true?

At last she's stopped buying pregnancy kits she spent a fortune on Clear Blue

She's too late for an abortion, is adoption
 the route she should go?

If only she'd worked things out earlier instead of being so slow
Why was she so scared to stop him? Why the hell was she so weak?

It's not as if she even likes him they very rarely speak!!!

She worries for her little sister now she's pregnant he leaves her alone

How she envies her friends at school they come from A Normal Home!!!

That's Life

IVF can have its problems

A smart looking couple on 4 both stare at the couple on 2

She whispers I won't be a minute love then she rushes off to the loo

She dabs her eyes with a tissue and instructs herself to be strong

This month it could really happen a baby could come along

She must try to be more positive have more faith in the IVF

Her Consultant said fingers crossed you 2 after running the final tests

He sees her coming back relieved the couple on 2 are long gone

He envies them with a passion ok love? we must carry on

Her parents don't really help they remind her your Sisters got 4

His patience is wearing thin now he dreads their knock on the door

He could do without their banter they should understand their pain

For most couples sex is spontaneous but for them it's a terrible strain

She keeps coming up with new remedies props her feet up all

Glimpses of Life

the next day

He bought her a new recliner chair there are times he could run away

His mums really understanding she helps them hold onto some hope

She tells them you must never give up
And it helps them both to cope

 She's papered the babies room the drawers are filled with baby clothes

But what if it doesn't happen? How will she cope? Heaven knows!!

He's not a nasty person but just look at that lady on 3

Hers are all different colours bet she shells em out like peas

Christ it's ok for some he thinks she stares at him dangling her keys

Wake up honey time we got back shall we try it with me on my knees?

He picks up the shopping and smiles she's worth it she's such a good wife

Let's hurry my temperatures dropping love it's no good complaining That's Life.

Joseph Their Darling Boy

The birth was relatively easy no forceps or complications

But the baby was whisked away without any explanations

After 13 years of waiting they felt it was very unkind

He called the midwife over can we see him? Would you mind?

You can but in a while Doctor needs a little chat

She could see they were both very anxious she gave both their hands a light pat

He stood at the foot of the bed his face was ashen and grey

He had to find the right words it was such a hard thing to say

Your son is very healthy 8lbs 2 is a very good weight

They searched his face for some clues frightened to hear their fate

Doctor please spit it out were so worried about our son

He hated this part of his job he felt tempted to turn and run

As I said before your sons healthy but sadly he's been born with Downs

It's a chronological disorder he avoids eye contact and frowns

The words hit them like a bombshell they stared at each other aghast

Glimpses of Life

She sobbed uncontrollable sobs he found his voice at long last

But we've waited for 13 years you must have made a mistake
Tell me I'm having a nightmare how much more do we have to take?

We've even re mortgaged our home to pay for the IVF

We've used every penny we've worked for there's barely anything left

He'd suggested that she had some tests to make sure that the babe was ok

But with a very small risk to the foetus she'd declined and decided to pray

I'll leave you 2 alone he said give you time to digest your news

I'll see you again tomorrow we'll discuss a few of your views

They stared at each other aghast unable to think or speak

He said shall we go to see him do you think you could take a peak?
She declined and faced the wall she shut up just like a clam

He tried so hard to get through and spent a fortune on the pram

His Mum was the first to see him she took hold of his tiny hand

She tried hard to convince them both he's a beautiful little man

He's a week old please go to see him what your doing is so very wrong

He so needs his Mummy and Daddy you really must try to be strong

I feel petrified she said he took hold of her trembling hand

His legs went to wobbly jelly he was barely able to stand

His tiny tongue was protruding under a mass of very black hair
They stared into the canvas cot he looked so helpless lying there

They got bolder and both held him close then they kissed his tiny head

Slowly coming to terms his got hair just like yours she said

He looks almost perfect she said just look at his fingers and toes

To be honest you wouldn't know he was downs when his little eyes are closed

By the time he'd reached 3 years old they were used to people staring

The more they did they found the more they ended up caring.

If only people realized that ALL children bring their own joy

No child could be loved more than Joseph they call him 'Their Darling Boy'

Just Coming Mother Dear

Not all Mum's are nice

The librarian look alike on 12 wears her hair in a bun

Shares a home with a tabby called Molly and her extremely dominant Mum

Her brogues are made by Clarkes her clothes are from Bhs

And ever since she left school she's worked for the DSS

She's bought Mum some lavender water with a miracle it might raise a smile

They take weekend breaks in Blackpool close to the golden mile

It breaks her heart to leave Molly she regularly sheds a tear

Mum tells her she's being pathetic it's only 4 times a year

Mum hates it that Molly's so pampered and allowed to sleep on her bed

Always hairs on the pillows overweight and overfed

She counts 7 tins of Whiskas that's a large one for every day

You'll kill that creature with kindness it could die while were away

She wonders why she's so spiteful she desperately misses her Dad

He shared her love for Molly she thinks of the cuddles they

had

He died from cancer last Christmas he just got smaller then wasted away

She prayed hard for God to spare him constantly night and day

She feels warm when she thinks of her Father the checkout girls voice brings her back

That will be £5 20 please and could she please hurry and pack

She puts it all into her basket perched on the front of her bike

Her legs become a blur god she wonders what Mum will be like

She's watching TV as usual this is rubbish and your half an hour late

Your dinners in the oven by now it's stuck to the plate

I haven't seen a soul all day loneliness is like a disease

She wonders why she lies so much and why she's so hard to please

She knows that a neighbour calls in they moan to one another

If only she had a sister to help or even an older brother

Molly purrs round her ankles ok baby it won't be long

While you're at it make me some tea not like piddle now make mine strong

Glimpses of Life

Oh and make my hot water bottle then put it into my bed

Oh and get me 2 Nurofen tablets I've got a terrible head

It's ok for you out working I don't see a soul all day long

Have you made that cup of tea yet? And don't forget make it strong!!!

You can run my bath in a while and my toenails need cutting again

There's some washing on the line and it looks very much like rain

She buries her head in the cat and produces a salty tear

Molly starts licking it off 'Just Coming Mother Dear'.

The Right Move

She wanted a man just like dad

Why can't Mother understand she keeps saying it was only a
cat

She can't help the way she's feeling Mum keeps sniggering
silly bat

She totally blames herself it's my fault Molly ran under that
car

She should have kept her in or not let her wander so far

She gathered her up in her arms the car driver stood there and
stared

She was fumbling around for her mobile she'd never felt quite
so scared

But it was far too late for a vet poor Molly had met her death

Used up her precious 9th life taken her last shallow breath

She sobbed uncontrollable sobs she was totally out of control

He wrapped his coat round her shoulders whispering come on
dear it's cold

He escorted her back to her Mothers she screamed at her what
is it now?

She seemed extra evil that evening he thought to himself
wicked cow

You should have been more careful you've only yourself to

blame

As if she didn't feel bad enough would she ever get over the shame?

They buried her in the back garden under the willow tree

Mother made nasty remarks you can save all those tears for me

He made Molly a headstone carved it himself out of stone

She looked forwards to his visits she didn't feel quite so alone

Mother was incredibly jealous she kept saying he's not for you

He's not very good looking either he's got a big nose like a Jew

His eyes are too close together that means he's prone to telling lies

But she decided to use her own judgement deep down she was very wise

They found they had lots in common their love for animals for a start

She grew to like him a lot like Dad he had a kind heart

He'd ring her at work every lunchtime bought her flowers every weekend
He was kind and understanding and an honest and faithful friend

A month after Molly passed on he gave her a bundle one

morning

A beautiful tabby kitten he said it's time to stop mourning

They set up home together although Mother didn't approve

He was so much like her Father so she knew that she'd made

The Right Move

Who'd be a GP

The harassed GP on 11 has a job to remember their names

For years he's coped with the wingers and he's sick of their aches and pains

He checks his watch yet again the surgery's about to start

 Mr Thingmees the first one today worrying about his heart

He's been for 3 ECG'S in a year, what will it take to convince him?

How can he make things more clear?

Another bloody hypochondriac to add to his long list

No wonder he's got a problem it helps a lot getting pissed

Mr em oo ja ma flip will be next as a faker he's the best

He'll be after another sick note to give to the DSS

Back trouble that's always a good one it's so very hard to prove

He'll come in doubled right over saying Doc I can ardly move

There's no point in calling his bluff he's been faking it now for years

He truly believes it himself and he often produces real tears

His neighbours call him Noel Coward he should win a best Actor gong

But claiming the money is his divine right he has no idea that it's wrong

Next will be Mrs um thingermy trouble with her plates of meat

Stands her stick by the door ok doc if I take a seat?

Of course my dear he'll reply now tell me how have you been?

I don't like to be a killjoy doc but I don't think much of your cream!!!

Then there's Miss what's her name? Infections down you know where

He reluctantly pulls on his glove s that's right dear you lay down there

Lay back dear and open wide just let your knees fall apart

I fought I was in the dentist's doc he thinks to himself silly tart

How many times must he warn her? He's been clearing this up for years

But if he speaks to her harshly she runs out in a flood of tears
He envies the checkout girl he'd far sooner do her job

The money might be very poor but at least he'd be rid of this mob

Next will be Mrs Oo Ja Ma Flip with her revolting daughter Nadine

Glimpses of Life

He needs to syringe her ears again and last time they were none too clean

Mrs Oo Ja Ma Flip makes excuses poor lambs been ever so sick

If he could unleash his feelings he'd give her fat arse a good kick

Nadine is such a winger she cries at the drop a hat

Spoilt rotten by the whole family over indulged and extremely fat

She came along in the change of life Mr Oo Ja Ma Fip said heavens above
But Nadine is such an angel they've surrounded her now with love

She left School at Christmas last year and she loves being home with her mum

She buys piles of Women's magazines and sits around all day on her bum

She records the Jeremy Kyle shows and watches them night and day

I feel so sorry for these people mum she's often heard to say

She never looks for a job they tell her it doesn't matter

Just like Dad she collects her cheque and stays at home getting fatter and fatter

Then there's Mr Em Thinger Me Bob he's always so very down

He's tried many anti depressants yet he still wears a permanent frown

His wife left him years ago she grew sick of his miserable ways

She ran off with his brother John he'd show her happier days

She didn't understand depression thought he could just pull himself together

She'd say he's just bloody miserable there's no chance of us staying together

The doctor thinks of his home life the kids have both left home

His wife bores him half to death but it's better than living alone

His nurse would love an affair the one that does the injections

But after he's seen all the wingers he doubts he could raise an erection

He's thought of trying Viagra but there's always the side effects
He'd rather give drugs a miss and not worry about being erect

His nurse tries every trick in the book fishnet stockings and high heeled shoes

She's always making suggestions at times she's down right crude

Sometimes he gets a bit aroused but the bottle does far more good

Glimpses of Life

Sends him off into oblivion and deadens his sexual mood

He imagines shooting his patients or giving their necks a good throttle

The only thing that helps him to cope? The saviour he's found in a bottle

Then there's poor Mr What's His Name? He's fading pretty fast

His complexion is pallid and sour see you next time Doc if I last!!!
But Mr What's His Names always cheerful he puts the others to shame

They should take a leaf from his book Christ why can't they all be the same!!!!!!!!!

Will that pretty young girl turn up the one who is deep in the shit?

He keeps telling her don't waste your money on clear blue pregnancy kits

People think his life is a breeze I wish I earned half his wage

If only they knew what it's like for GP's sometimes he gets in a rage

In the glove box lurks his saviour swigs some down as he drives along

By the time he reaches the surgery his saviour is empty all gone.

Away On Their Toe's

Youth is wasted on the young

She'd had 3 by the time she was 20 all fathered by different men

 She put it about a lot with anyone way back then

The sensible lads wouldn't touch her never knew where she'd been

They called her Lucy Elastic if you can see what I mean

She's aged 20 years in a decade once she was pretty and bright

But once she was sexually active she'd stay out most of the night

She acquired a taste for Jack Daniels and would often get into a brawl

On Thursdays she'd pick up her dole cheque and in no time was having a ball

She's been used by life's abusers she'd have liked a neat little home

Hates living in cement city what's the betting she'll end up alone

They all duffed her up and left her did none of them ever care?

It's made her all bitter and twisted Jesus this life's so unfair

Glimpses of Life

2 of them are sitting in prison neither knows he's a Dad

She's always had a strange attraction for men who turn out bad

She wonders who fathered who one of the Fathers was black

She looks for clues in their faces - could have been Bob Joe or Jack

She struggles with shopping from Asda the kids trail behind her like ducks

Hungry tired and fretful God she thinks life really sucks

Her Mother tried hard to warn her because her life had gone the same way

But youth is wasted on the young now she's got a high price to pay

History repeats itself her dad treated her mum just the same

Mum ended up in a similar plight and still tries to hide her shame

She dreams of meeting a millionaire who'll treat her like a princess

Odds on she meets more losers and her life becomes more of a mess

Her luck won't run to the Lottery because that's just not the way her life goes

She's been used by life's abusers then they had it 'Away On Their Toes'.

The Last Laugh

This one is about me and a very arrogant boss I had th[e] misfortune to work for. Every word of this is true, but he final[ly] got his comeuppance

The Warehouse Manager on 13 loves to shout at his staff

Moral is terribly low they've forgotten how to laugh

He thrives on feeling important and loves his company car

No Fords for the general manager he adores his convertible Saab

If you should happen to park in his place you'll find out how important he is

He's sacked staff for being too fat so he'd surely sack you for this

The postman parked in his reserved place he reported him to his boss

He swore at the postman tried to make him look small the bastard don't give a toss

He loves to play to an audience gets more pleasure and feels bigger still

He doesn't consider his workers even though he has made some of them ill

He gets pleasure from this abuse he loves to watch them squirm

One day he'll have them in order if it kills him he'll make

them learn

His ego is so enormous he must feed it all of the time

Abuse on a daily basis and then his ego is fine

He sees the Warehouse as his empire without him it would all fall down
But something might happen one day and the king will lose his crown

Then at last he got his come uppance and he lost his Ivory Tower

They put him behind a desk with no pension no staff and no power

The moral of this story? Don't disrespect your staff

There's always someone ready to fight back and it's he who gets The Last Laugh

Jealous Nasty And Greedy

If only we could see ourselves as others

The lady on checkout 2 is out shopping with her friend

They love a jolly good gossip but nothing that would offend

Her at 4's got new nets have you seen them?

That's the 3rd lot she's put up this year

Don't think much of the quality though you can tell they weren't very dear

I see he's bought a new car cheap skates it's only a Ford

That car properly sums that lot up it's all they can afford

She tells me their going away soon I'm sure she said it was Spain
Let's hope they don't all get the trots aye and experience terrible pain

Have you seen their new 3 piece suite it's nauseatingly green

She took me round to see it thinks she's the bloody queen

The shape of the bloody woman can she possibly get any thinner?

The bloody kids are like matchsticks that's baked beans on toast for dinner

Their brats are so bloody spoiled computers TV'S in their rooms

Glimpses of Life

She bought him a new Cam Corder pans, and tilts, and zooms

I'm so glad were nothing like them we wouldn't want to be

Were much nicer more pleasant people just like that lot should be
Have you seen their hot tub? With its plasma TV screen

He looks dreadful in his trunks his pot belly's such a scream

I'd hate to be like them though materialistic prats

Did you see them go out on Saturday dressed up to the nines with the brats?

She's working at Mc'donalds I find that really funny

He works in insurance they'd do anything for money

 What's that you said their moving oh great that's all we need

We all know they've got their faults but they've been known to do a good deed

Let's hope the new lot are like us aye? Pleasant friendly less needy

Not like that lot at number 4 – 'Jealous, Nasty, And Greedy

The Desperate Yo Yo Queen

Dieting don't you just hate it?

The overweight lady on checkout 6 can't wait to get home today

Her bags are filled with fresh cream cakes she takes out her purse to pay

The Yo Yo queen stares at the cream then serves up another portion

She blames it all on her ex he insisted she had the abortion

The Yo Yo queen has tried really hard to curb her huge addiction

She knows that her life is out of control she spends far too much time in the kitchen

She stuffs her self with chocolate Mars and Bountys and kit kats

King size bars of dairy milk then she tells herself she's not fat

She really adores a Dona Kebab Pizzas Burgers and Chips

She closes her eyes in ecstasy as she puts the food up to her lips

She's tried every trick in the diet books potions exercise pills

She's even tried speed to suppress the hunger but she ended up mentally ill

She'll eat a whole pack of chocolate digestives with her

morning cup of tea

Then she strips off and stares in the mirror cries and says poor me!!!!

She often eats for England more than enough for 2

Then she stuffs 2 fingers down her throat and runs to the nearest loo
She purges her stomach with laxatives at least 5 times a week

She spends the next day in agony feeling giddy and weak

She tried Colonic Irrigation where they put a pipe up your bum

She only lost 2 pounds in weight but it cost a tidy sum

She dreams of winning some money then she could go for a Gastric Band

Then she'd lose the weight in an instant and find herself a new man

Her friends don't really know the truth they think she's quite a scream

She's fat and happy they often say not a 'Desperate Yo Yo Queen'

The Under Cover Policeman

They say everyone has a secret

The policeman on checkout 16 is feeling a little fraught
He's got an enormous secret and he's scared of getting caught

He works for the SAS extremely cloak and dagger

He's very proud of his job and he walks with a permanent swagger

But the undercover policeman is more under cover than you think

If his colleagues knew his secret it would certainly cause a stink

But he keeps it all secretly secret extremely under wraps

Even his best friends don't know they'll find out one day perhaps

He awaits an important assignment an extremely dangerous job

He knows with the turn of a corner he could get a gun in his gob

He'll give the bastards what for show them he's hard as nails

Yet the thought of his secret leaking can make his complexion pale

He'll often polish his medals his chest puffs up with pride

But god if they knew his secret he feels like jelly inside

Glimpses of Life

He's off to Gaza next Thursday with the valiant SAS

He won't even get the jitters he copes very well with the stress

My private life is my business but it's bound to get out one day

Bet I know what your thinking the undercover policeman is gay

Sorry to tell you you're wrong this will probably make your hair curl

But he's had the operation the Policeman was born a girl

Lace

The undercover Policeman's Mum has never quite come to terms

To her he's still her Daughter and the thought of the op makes her squirm

She told the Neighbours her Daughter is dead an accident in a car

Her new Son was very angry how could she take things that far?

Why can't she accept what he's done he's been trapped in this body for years

Scared to tell others his secret crying his lonely tears

He's suffered incredible pain just to feel he knows who he is

If only people could understand life would be so much better than this

At last he's true to himself and he's well aware that life won't be easy
His battle with the stigma often makes him feel shaky and queasy

Why can't people accept who I am?
can't they see that it's hard being me?

As a child I knew the truth its taken years to be free

His Father quite surprised him though after getting over the shock

Glimpses of Life

It seems so strange to me Jo he said but   I'm used to you in a
frock

Your Mum will come round given time just try to give her
some space

She'll slowly get used to the jackboots and you were never
one for 'Lace.'

Roll On Bloody Death

Drugs who needs them?

The 3 druggies on checkout 2 all have a story to tell

They stick together like glue on their separate journeys to hell

Broken down veins like road maps eyes sunken deep in his head

Black shadows lurking beneath them a stomach that's rarely fed

The crack house is just like a tip strewn with super brew cans

Empty messy and sad just like well laid plans

He dreams of raising a family a semi in a tree lined street

But he hasn't a pot to piss in or decent shoes on his feet

He steals from the houses he dreams of to pay for the Ecstasy Along with the smack and the heroin god will he ever be free?

4 years ago you wouldn't have known him he owned a smart flat and a car

A job in the Stock Exchange but drugs have dragged him this far

So beware of becoming a druggie and cherish the freedom you've got

Don't touch the smack or the heroin don't even sample the pot

He drags himself up from the mattress muttering under his

breath

Time to go on a trip and Roll on Bloody Death..

Georgina Wakefield

The Top of the Pile

His mate Billy on checkout 5 has been on the hard stuff for years

His family disowned him ages ago got sick of crying their tears

Ecstasy, now there's a name for it Jesus that's really profound

When he made up his mind to sample it he should have booked his plot in the ground

It can boil your blood it can scramble your brain and unless you're lucky you'll go insane

He grubs around to pay for it just like a sewer rat

Lining the dealers pocket big fat evil rich cat

He even robbed his Mother to quell the craving inside

She finally gave up hope she'd tried and tried and tried

Dirty disposed of syringes lie broken on his stairs

He sidles up to his dealer whose more than willing to sell him his wares

He roars off in his Jag whispering loser under his breath

Now and again he has a good laugh when he hears of a premature death

But for now he's flying high diamonds behind his eyes

Soars like a golden eagle till he reaches the clear blue skies

Glimpses of Life

With a thud he'll hit the ground then back to reality

The tears will sting his eyes yet again but will he ever be free?

And tomorrow what of tomorrow back to playing the same old game?

He'll stare at his punctured arms then struggle to find a vein

So don't be tempted by drugs value the life that you've got

Or you could end up in the same boat On The Top Of The Pile To Rot......

Her Inner Light

The gaunt looking girl on 4 trails behind them near the till

She can't even remember a normal life just a massive habit to fill

On the streets by the age of 16 to pay for her craving for drugs

She mixes with the low life loser' dealers and thugs

She says the worst parts the smell of the ones that are none too clean

She'd much sooner deal with an ugly one its hard to imagine the scene

She's abused to feed her habit just like a human spitoon

Her favourites are the premmies at least it's over soon

She shoves the notes down her bra muttering poor sad sod

Tells herself that was the last time cross her heart she swears it to god

Her inner voice mocks till the next time that the craving proves far too strong

Give her 2 days at the most then correct me if I'm wrong

She showers vigorously to try to get rid of the smell

The first time she laughed and sampled a joint began her journey to hell

Christ the horrors of drugs there's far more to life than this

Glimpses of Life

There's decency there's happiness instead of a deep dark abyss

But for her there's misery and craving there's sunken bloodshot eyes
There's depression as bad as it gets along with a few phoney highs

Once she was really attractive she was lively vivacious and bright

Till the day she decided to sample some pot then out went ' Her Inner Light'

People with Schizophrenia

Time to Change

Stigma is still a massive problem in Society. But this is the year 2010 the age of technology. We are way behind when it comes to educating the public. When in Gods name will things change? This incident actually happened to my own son [and my family] Time 2 Change is the name for the 4 year Rethink campaign aimed at tackling Stigma. My family took part in a video to secure the lottery money [18 million pounds] for this campaign. Rethink actually re enacted this painful incident using an actor to play the part of our Son

The Leisure Pool Manager on 1 saw a young man having a swim

He comes to the pool quite frequently he decided to question him

The young man has a mental illness he's been suffering now for years

The Managers quite unaware of all this oblivious to all of our tears

One of the staff asked him questions as to why he stayed in there so long

He tells them about his condition he tells them he needs to get strong

For years he laid in bed due to lack of motivation

He wanted to build up his muscles life is hard when you take medication

Glimpses of Life

A week later he's called out of the pool 2 uniformed officers in wait

They ask him some very strange questions which put him in quite a state

Why did they ask him about children? As if he were a paedophile

This was so far from the truth their suggestions were evil and vile

A Head Teacher had called the Police she was worried about the kids

I asked her what was my son doing? Explain to me what he did?

He'd just been truthful about his illness and all hell broke loose that day

Nobody understood but my but Son had the price to pay

He wouldn't go swimming again he couldn't face it he said

This incident made him ill things kept running around his head

The message in this story is about lack of education

It's badly affected the family and added to our frustration
My Son was deeply depressed anti depressants for the next year

When we recall this incident we always shed a tear

I feel ashamed Mum he'd say his shame borne of their

ignorance

Yet this is the year 2010 to me it just doesn't make sense

We must all keep chipping away we must educate the media

Till at last we gain some respect for 'People With Schizophrenia'

Free

Carers save this country an estimated 87.4 billion pounds a year

The couple on checkout 9 have a very autistic son

Their lives are terribly hard there are times that they both want to run

He's thrashing around on the floor people are rude they just stare

Some even make rude remarks but their past the point that they care

She remembers the day he was born life was so different then

The years haven't passed very quickly yet by September 4th he'll be 10

She ponders about the future how will they stand the pace?

The strain is often too much he used to be quite a case

It's taken its toll on his humour his workmates say he's just not the same

He'd like to see how they would cope It's enough to drive you insane

She gently takes hold of his hand come on love lets take this lad home

He's still on the floor throwing tantrums he feels comforted by her tone

He hoists him up on his shoulders come on son it's time for
tea

Their held tightly together by loyalty both wishing sometimes
they were 'free.'

Such a Farce

The perils of alcohol

The lady on checkout 4 buys some booze though she knows it's wrong

Tells herself this is the last time and that she must try to be strong

She's promised to join AA as she's done many times in the past

He's given her too many chances the next one will be the last

He's sick of the drunken stupours sick of the smell of the booze

Bored with the house being dirty and tired of feeling abused

She's always hiding the bottles whisky rum and gin

She covers them up with papers hides them all in the bin

He arranges posh dinner parties lays them
on for his clients
She's forced to mix with working class snobs so she drinks in stony defiance

She can see they've forgotten their roots she knows some of them from the past

They were brought up on Council Estates but their all moving up pretty fast

How can they forget where they've come from or the loo out the back in the yard

Some are ashamed of their families even though they had it real hard

She's found an escape in her drinking relief when she filled up each glass

But with time it became a habit and her life is 'Such A Farce'

Well Aware of the Grief

Never be ashamed of who we are

The young man on checkout 4 is feeling somewhat confused

He knows that it's high time he told them but he knows they won't be amused

Will his Father blow his stack? Mum will certainly throw a fit

His Brother will be disgusted he feels he's deep in the shit

He's sick of the nasty remarks its high time you settled down

He's lost count of the time he's heard it they both wear the same old frown

Christ your Brothers been married twice he's about to shack up with his third

Why can't you find a good woman we find it so absurd?

He'll say listen I do have a partner the only thing is he's a man

He knows it will do their heads in neither will understand

Dad will say Christ your a Builder son please tell me this isn't the truth

Mum will cry where did I go wrong?   Did something bad happen in your youth?

I know I longed for a daughter but I did bring you boys up the same

What on earth will the neighbours say how will we cope with the shame?

People will call you Nancy boy faggot Pansy and queer

Look your poor Mothers in tears now where the hell do we go from here?

Have you thought of talking to your GP it could be that you're unwell

Why don't they understand? They make his life bloody hell

He has to be true to himself why can't they just understand?

Instead of fancying a woman he just fancies a man

The thought of bedding a woman fills him with utter disgust

He tried very hard to deny it but in the end it was a must

He decides that today is the day with clenched muscles and gritted teeth

He knocks on the door rather loudly 'Well Aware of the Grief'.

An Important Role

Care workers deserve more money this one is based on my friend Sherry who truly cares about her work

The Care Worker on checkout 5 is shopping for clients again

There's 35 in her unit it's a wonder she's not insane

The Schoolteacher in resi 1 is suffering from Dementia no less

Her family rarely visit they just can't cope with the stress

Old Hetty on resi 2 doesn't have long for this world

She still applies her makeup and makes sure her hairs nicely curled

Hetty was once a teacher she really loved her job
Although he coped for a while it all got too much for Bob

When he comes he stares out of the window either that or he takes to reading

The Care Worker tries to talk to him she knows his heart is bleeding

She's really concerned about Dolly she really isn't so well

Her 2 daughters never visit they say they can't cope with the smell

Soldier Bill thinks he's still out there fighting she wipes the egg from his tie

When he talks about days gone by it brings a tear to her eye

She laid out old Jack this morning he'd been fading lately real fast

He was one of the nicer ones she's relieved he's at peace at last
Matron tells her she's far too slow her problem? You're far too kind

She worries about their bed sores and tries hard to ease their minds

Old Joe tries to touch her bum if he thinks he has half a chance

When it comes to their Social events he always asks her to dance

But she knows she'll never change this is her own kind way

The money she gets is paltry it's reflected in her pay

All that for £6 50 an hour and not exactly an easy job

She throws the stuff on the belt she's forgotten the soap for old Bob

She makes her way back through the crowds she knows it will worry his soul
She takes this job very seriously it's A Very Important Role

Keeping Her Cool

Being married to God is not always easy

She thinks of him night and day but the guilt is so hard to bear

She wishes they'd never met if only she didn't care

She knows what she's done is wrong she's forbidden to love him like this

She shivers inside with sheer pleasure as she recalls that very first kiss

He came to repair the boiler she bent down to pick up his spanner

He took it from her trembling hand her heart beating like a trip hammer

Their eyes met and both of them knew the attraction was too hard to resist

He cupped her face in his hands next came the first fateful kiss

It was over before it began seething unleashed passion

They tore the clothes from each other as if it might go out of fashion

She prayed to God for forgiveness cried out for guidance that night

Divided by different needs one sheer pleasure the other sheer fright

She tells herself that was the last time it must never happen again

The deceit too much to bare nothing is worth all that pain

He left his card on the table just in case he was needed once more

He kissed her tenderly then quietly closed the door
His workmates would never believe him yeah right they'd say a Nun?

I suppose she was really attractive nice face nice tits great bum?!!!

Please yourselves he'd say I swear to God it's no lie

I knew you wouldn't believe, but I didn't even have to try

Sister Josie how is the heating? Sister Beth's voice brought her round

The radiators appear to be hotter but it's making a very strange sound

Christ if Sister Beth knew the thought of it makes her freeze

She clasped her hands together then she fell down to her knees

If only she could put the clock back and start all over again
Will she ever be able to forgive herself how will she deal with the pain?

She'd given herself to God how could she have been such a fool

She hid the card under her habit she must try to Keep Her Cool

Life's A Funny Old Game

Money isn't everything

It glistened amongst the rubbish he held on to it tight in his pocket

To keep it safe till he arrived home at he thought he'd found a locket

It was a beautiful sovereign ring he could see it was very old

He marvelled at the detail it was heavy and made of gold

The next morning at Hatton Garden he got the shock of his life

He'd no longer be emptying bins he broke the good news to his wife

It was rare and worth a fortune priceless the jeweller said

Jesus I'm rich at last it kept going round his head

6 months later he lived in a mansion with a swimming pool in the yard

No need to scrimp and save he left a life that was terribly hard

Yet he missed all his mates on the bins young Robbie old Jock and Joe

He missed all the laughs that they shared the time went by terribly slow

He even missed the work his reason to get up out of bed

He felt there wasn't a purpose he was bored right out of his
head

He decided to go back to see them they thought the lottery
had brought him luck

They laughed when they saw the Rolls Royce they said where
there's money there's muck
They all envied him with a passion he envied them just the
same

He preferred his days as a Dustman 'life's a funny old game'.

Comfort at Last

Try as he might to stop last night he was gambling again

His wife is sick of the debts and the kids wearing hand me down clothes

He promises that was the last time but deep down inside he knows

He had it real hard as a child from the age of 7 he was abused

She has no idea what he's been through but he's always on a short fuse

Although he has this problem she loves him with all of her heart

She cannot face life without him but it seems their destined to part

How he wishes his life had been different he's in such emotional pain

The gambling brings him some relief again and again and again

It takes his mind off the past especially when he wins

His Father's got off very lightly and he'll never pay for his sins

If only his mind could escape from his futile painful past

Her Mother paid for a counsellor but he began to delve into his past

Glimpses of Life

He jumped up from the couch pretty sharpish and ran out of there pretty fast

He disappeared into the nearest bookies where he gets some comfort at last

The Psychiatric Nurse

Not the easiest of jobs

The CPN on checkout 5 is feeling extremely stressed

Her workload is far too big she's in desperate need of a rest

She doesn't have enough time for her clients the paperwork drives her insane

She'd much rather have the time to help with their mental pain

She finds them quite amazing for what they have to endure

It's just far too much red tape will she cope with it? She's not sure

She administers depot injections and dishes out many pills

She comforts the ones that cry and she listens to their ills
One of her patients is getting her down he suffers from Tourettes

The neighbours say he's just an animal and he needs to go to the vets

He swears and ticks and spits but his condition is way out of control

He hates this wretched condition and he wants to hide in a hole

The young girl with Anorexia gets thinner every day

Her parents have tried everything but she's simply wasting

away

Last week a young man didn't make it threw himself under a train

24 and he'd taken enough far too much mental pain

He suffered from Bi Polar and had done for too many years
His family had always stood by him and cried a river of tears

His poor Mother was distraught, she'd looked after him so well

But she understood him taking his life it was purely a living hell

She held her hand and cried with her she said it's an evil curse

She wonders how long she'll cope The Psychiatric Nurse.

Me or you

A test of faith

The vicar on checkout 6 is thinking of leaving the flock

He's losing his faith in God after a terrible shock

His baby at 4 years old has lost her fight with leukaemia

An angelic blonde headed angel adored by all who'd seen her

His life is falling apart it's been such a terrible strain

He prayed that God would spare her over and over again

2 long years she had suffered a few times they thought she'd won

How can he comfort his wife or explain to his 6 year old son

His wife's slowly falling apart she just sits by the window staring

Their divided by their situation the pain is too deep to be sharing

He knows it's a test of his faith but he doesn't know if he'll pull through

Would we still believe in God if this happened to me or you?.

Side by Side

This next one is about my sister and a very arrogant Heart Surgeon and this actually happened

True Love

The lady on 2 in a wheelchair desperately needs a new heart

She's been waiting now for 4 long years 4 years of falling apart

You need a heart the old ones rotten her Consultants words never forgotten

He just came out with it just like that no compassion just matter of fact

As if it were a tomato not her precious heart

What a wonderful bedside manner she thought not exactly a very good start

To a relationship that should be special in circumstances as hard as this

Her fragile sensitive feelings sent into a deep dark abyss

If you want to join my hall of fame you'll have to lose 3 stone

They stared down at her from the surgery walls she felt so lost and alone

The Consultant drives a Bentley shiny large and smart

It matches his persona she could see that from the start

The number plate reads ONE BIG 1 aptly fitting for him

He wears his greens and his boots even when there's no ops booked in

She understands that he's clever and that he's almost playing God
But that doesn't give him the right to be such an arrogant sod

She thinks about the cost of a transplant finances play a big part
Not exactly cheap to replace somebody's heart

Sometimes it all overwhelms her and it often makes her cry

She knows what it means if she gets one somebody else has had to die

She remembers a song from the past [anyone who had a heart]

She shudders at its enormity hers immediately starts to beat fast

Tomorrow they're off to Papworth she'll endure the many tests

Will a new heart be on the horizon or will they say she must rest

Her husband takes hold of her hand to prepare for the next bumpy ride

They face their journey together love keeping them side by side.

Christmas Past

Heart warming

The elderly man on 5 is dreading the festive season

His wife died from a stroke last Christmas so you could say he has a good reason

He dreads the trees and the holly he hates all that food and booze

Drinking and gorging for days just gives you more weight to lose

He's really in need of some money has an interview at a large store

It was advertised as person required so he doesn't know what it's for

The store manager said you will be perfect he'd hardly had time to speak

Your costume is here in that box could you make a start Friday week?

He peered into the box furtively inside was a Santa Suit

 Some false snow in a carrier bag a white beard a sack and black boots

He really needed the money so he reluctantly tried it all on

Took comfort that he would be richer he shouted out loud oh what fun

He started as planned on the Friday after practising ho ho ho

Surrounded by luminous reindeers knee deep in fluffy white snow

The children all seemed to love him their excitement kept him going

He told the kids to make a wish that on Christmas day it's snowing

He loves the look on their faces hands and feet all aglow

His life took on a new meaning his time went by fast not slow

He found that he really enjoyed it and began wishing his job would last

He's promised to come back next year for the magic of 'Christmas Past'.

Looking After Mum

Some Carers are far too young

The young lad on checkout 1 is nearly 12 years of age

He feels like running away things have finally reached this stage

He's old before his time for 2 years he's been a carer

His mum suffers from MS and he wishes life had been fairer

His dad went after a year just upped and left one cold day

His mum cried for a whole week he didn't know what to say

The wheelchair did it for Dad just seemed to be the last straw

Shacked up with some slag round the corner she's either got 3 kids or 4

How could he just up and leave them? After all those happy years

He hates his dad now with a vengeance his anger brings him to tears

He gets her up and helps her get dressed he puts her to bed at night

Sometimes she threatens to end it all and he's terrified that she might

Her speech has become very slurred he can't understand what she's saying

On top of all that moneys tight it's not much DSS are paying

He's got behind with his schoolwork he's always tired out

His teacher keeps asking him questions he wishes she'd just butt out

He dreams of a normal childhood football, computer games

His Mother calls from the bedroom I'm in need of the toilet James.

There's a pizza in the freezer lad that will do for our tea

He dreams of enjoying his life dreams of being free

Could you bring in my foot spa after tea they could really do with a soak

And while your up could you see to the fire the coals could do with a poke

His mate knocks and asks him out there's a game on the rec wanna come?

I keep telling you Mark I'm a carer and I have to look after my mum

The Perfect Wife

More Secrets

The lady on checkout 2 appears perfect in every way

She takes out her soft leather purse and patiently waits to pay

Her nails are perfectly manicured her suit is a lovely fit

Her shoes are the finest leather but they do pinch her toes a bit

Her home is much the same equipped with the best right through

Carpets that you could sink into a suite made of Hyde in dark blue

He's always wanted a child but she's never felt the need

Besides it could spoil their home and she's too engrossed in her greed

She drives a Mercedes sports car has it polished religiously each week

Her best friend's son spilled his cola she slapped him and now they don't speak

He buys her whatever he can gives in to her every whim

He knows her through and through but does she really know him?

He finds his relief elsewhere she's nothing like his wife

In fact their like chalk and cheese she leads a different life

He pays for the service he gets and to her it's simply a job

But its better than working at Woolies and brings in a tidy few bob

She doesn't jump up when its over she's not bothered by the crease in the sheets

The perfect wife polishes the taps he escapes for a while and cheats.

He wonders why he stays with her he's sick to death of the moans

He convinces himself it's not that bad and it's better than being alone

She's not grateful for all the material things she's not happy with her life

He mutters miserable bitch but she thinks she's the perfect wife

The Lady On Checkout 8

Relationships who'd have them?

The lady on checkout 8 desperately needs a man

Someone to share her life someone to hold her hand

She's tried various dating agencies she has some funny stories to tell

Only one was passable the others were truly hell

She arranged to meet one in town he turned up in a mustard suit

She noticed his wooden leg and swiftly gave him the boot

A dark headed one she quite fancied had problems with his toupee

It fell off in the mushroom soup whilst enjoying a meal one day

The waitress let out a scream thinking it was a giant spider

She fell about in fits as she watched his parting get wider

Another one seemed quite nice but she wondered why he didn't smile

When he did he had one tooth at the front she felt like running a mile

Her best mate said looks aren't everything she agreed with her in theory

But at the end of the day they help and by now she was getting weary

A ginger one who seemed ok had some very strange hobbies and habits

She felt they'd got nothing in common he loved hiking-measured rainfall - bred

rabbits

The next one had lost his wife her photos were everywhere

She found it rather off-putting he didn't seem to care

Talked about nothing else tried to change her into his wife

They argued about this problem she told him to get a life

She's given it up as a very bad job she finally got in a state

She's brought herself a parrot the lady on checkout 8.

So Mean

We are all Gods children

The corner shopkeeper on 5 is checking up on his stock

He feels like jelly inside almost ready to blow his top

He's invested in solid steel shutters and expensive burglar alarms

Yet still they manage to hurt him they take pleasure in causing him harm

They daubed his shop with cruel slogans like PAKKI it's time to go home

He's sick and tired from all the worry he feels so very alone

He doesn't ask for trouble by nature he's passive and kind

His wife's on a psychiatric ward they've told him she's losing her mind

The fire bomb was the worst thing took months and months to repair

Her light seemed to go out that night she just didn't seem to care

His children get bullied at School they call them names throw stones pull their hair

The youngest one keeps crying it's really so unfair

He's done all he can to stop it everything in his power

Life has become a nightmare that gets worse with every hour

He'd love to back to his country he's also aware that's a dream

He buries his head in his hands and wonders why they are 'So Mean.'

The Driving Instructor

Not always an easy job

The driving school instructor on 7 is often frightened to death

He swears some of them are out to kill him they want him to take his last breath

The lesson at 2 was terrifying like going round a race track, a boy racer at 17

He told him DON'T EVER COME BACK!!!

Unlike the lady at 4 the car didn't leave the kerb

 She burst into floods of tears it was really quite absurd

He swears the one at 6pm had something wrong with her sight

She just didn't see that van he nearly got into a fight

The van driver wasn't amused said he needed a dog and a stick

He was built like giant haystacks so he got out of there pretty quick

Last month he met the worst one she'd failed her 24th test

Braked on a busy dual carriageway and said that she needed to rest

He lost his temper and shouted she freaked and jumped out of the car

She ended up with both legs in plaster this time it pushed him too far

It does have its compensations though especially when it's hot

The young girls don't wear much these days he gets to see what they've got

He's known as a patient man mostly manages to keep his cool

But he's thinking of changing his job he's sick of the driving school.

All Over Again

Life isn't always easy for Junior Doctors

The Student Doctor on 7 has been up again all night

Doubled up on his shift he's aware that this isn't right

He's scared that he'll make a mistake he knows they are easily made

He sees himself in the window Jesus he needs a good shave

He feels it's so wrong what he's doing but knows there isn't really a choice

But what if one of them croaks it? Mocks his negative inner voice

His girlfriend left him last week she'd taken enough at long last

Shed forgotten the last time they'd socialised as for sex that was back in the past

When he studied at medical school he'd no idea it would end up like this

He recalls the fun that they had the times they went out and got pissed

His parents are really proud of him they encourage him to carry on

His mum brags to the neighbours he's a Doctor you know my son

His brothers got it so easy he's a fishmonger the lucky sod

All he has to worry about is where to buy the best cod

He wanted to be a DJ regrets wasting this precious life

At this rate he'll never settle down have a home a family a wife
He gratefully climbs into bed after setting the alarm for 10

Yet another doubler tonight and it'll start all over again.

Glimpses of Life

For Most of Us

Some people love the work they do

The Vet on checkout 3 is wearing a troubled frown

He has to explain to old Alice that he has to put Bobby down

She's 80 Bobby's 17 her constant companion for years

He knows it will break her heart he's prepared for many tears

Bobby's crippled with arthritis it's really the only way out

It's pitiful now to watch him struggling to get about

He delivered a calf on Wednesday in lashings of torrential rain

On Friday he put a racehorse to sleep it fell in a race and was lame

He fondly remembers his childhood always knew he'd be a Vet

He was born with this love for Gods creatures always surrounded by pets

He knows it has it's problems but the good bits outweigh all of that

Just to see the love for her kittens displayed by a Mother cat

He knows that he's one of the lucky ones he truly enjoys what he does

It's not just a means to an end as work is for most of us.

Lost Years

If only springs to mind

A lady on checkout 9 feels that life is full of regrets

She often feels bitter and angry and she hankers for more than she
gets

Her Daughter is really pretty she envies her golden hair

She'd have loved to look like she does life just isn't fair

She pays for the tanning parlours a manicurist for her nails

Buys her clothes from top designer stores and she never buys from
sales

She buys her beautiful underwear fishnet stockings and high heeled
shoes

She's a Beauty Queen and locally she's often in the news

Her daughter got really excited at the sight of her new padded bra

Hubby told her you've lost your mind this time you've gone too far

For Christmas she wanted a Pole Dancing outfit complete with
fishnet tights

Mum obliged as always she never puts up a fight

She always wanted this type of life but it didn't come her way

She works at the local bookies for quite a meagre pay

She encourages her daughter constantly tells that she's a winner

Glimpses of Life

She runs her around sometimes for miles and tells her she needs to get thinner

She rows with hubby constantly he tells her this just isn't good

Christ she's only just 7 years old and what about a childhood?

He knows she's fulfilling her own dreams and this will only lead to tears

He can't believe her mentality and what about the 'Lost Years'

The Social Worker on checkout 2

Life is full of regrets

The Social Worker on checkout 2

Keeps thinking about the tribunal

She keeps going over her huge mistakes

Friday next is the babies funeral
He was just coming up to a year

How could she have been so blind?

She was there to protect him

She was there to be kind

His injuries were appalling

She sees his face all the while

His blue blue eyes haunt her very soul

How did he still manage to smile?

But she'd scurried back to her own kids

She'd kissed them both goodnight

How could she ignore his pain?

How could she ignore his plight?

Why was she so unfeeling?

Glimpses of Life

Was she blind? Or was she deaf?

Perhaps she'd lost her sense of smell

She'd missed the stench of death

She detests herself she lies awake

How could she have left him alone?

Will she ever be able to forgive herself?

I'm a mortgage payer ~ a clone

But her family has to eat that's why she'd come out today

She keeps thinking of emigrating miles and miles away

Why did she trust his Mother?

Or her evil partner in crime?

She's obsessed with the same old thoughts

Round and round her exhausted mind

She wakes up from a fitful sleep

Dreading the thought of the day

She rarely goes out of the house

She's suspended from work on half pay

She can feel the fingers pointing at her

People hate her for what she **didn't** do

If only she'd done her job properly

The Social Worker on checkout 2

Love Can Conquer All

And it often does

The young woman on checkout 3 feels fearful confused and sad

She knows she has to face it he won't be the husband she had

His burns are quite extensive 75% maybe more

She wished he'd never signed up wonders what's this bloody   war for?

His mum said it was what he wanted a soldier through and through

His dreams were already cemented before he ever met you

She was often really quite spiteful and jealous of what they had

She'd always felt far closer and more at ease with his dad

She took a deep breath as she entered the ward then she looked right into his eyes

His voice was barely a whisper how do you like my disguise?

He was swathed in cream crepe bandages covered up from head to toe

The nurse said please don't stay too long he's feeling rather low

How can you ever love me he said I look like an ugly freak

My face will look repulsive she found her voice to speak

I'd love you no matter what she said she took hold of his badly burned hand

Love can conquer anything even though this is not what w
planned

You're still my wonderful Joe she said our love will see us throug

His eyes misted over with unshed tears he said I don't deserve you

His mother entered the room and blurted I can look after my son

You won't have to do that Mother he said love had conquered ar
won

Life can be very difficult and sometimes we take a fall

But if we truly care for each other 'Love Simply Conquers All'

Queen of the Wags

Money Money Money

The girl on checkout 1 is known as queen of the wags

She's often seen in designer shops laden down with carrier bags

She's married to a footballer he plays for Chelsea no less

He gives her anything she wants he'll pay £5000 for one dress

She drives a Jaguar convertible her teeth are whiter than white

She carries a tiny Chihuahua he's often been known to bite

The dogs just another possession a designer accessory

She adores him she's named him PRADA parades him for all to see

She jets off to Paris once a week she's obsessed by HELLO and OK

She's so impressed with the Beckham's can't wait to meet them one day

She strives to look just like Victoria she's my hero she tells her friends

She scans every magazine she can find to follow all of her trends

Her home is extremely opulent leopard skin rugs pure crystal galore

An Olympic sized swimming pool Jacuzzi and Sauna but she still wants so much more

She sticks her nose in the air at the beggars she passes by

She never questions their plight she never wonders why?

She wouldn't spare them a penny they deserve all that they get

Her bloke earns at least ninety grand a week for kicking a ball in net

If only she could understand that everything can't be bought

One day will she realise that life's not about what she thought?

Will she see that it doesn't matter if someone is dressed in rags?

Then she won't be impressed by possessions and she won't 'Queen Of The Wags'

OCD 123

A very painful condition

The Footballer with the queen of the wags suffers from OCD

His mind is often in turmoil he dreams of being free

He taps on the counter hundreds of times he counts 123 456

He's sick to death of the rituals and his mind being ruled by tricks

He washes his hands time after time then he washes them once again

He'd give every penny he's got, to be normal instead of insane

He stares at the cans in the cupboards stacks them neatly all in a row

It takes up so much of his time if only this curse would go

He knows she suspects something's wrong keeps giving him very strange glances

He's scared to tell her about it he'd rather not take any chances

She's not really understanding although she's great at spending his cash

She looks so good on his arm though when he takes her to a bash

If his secret ever gets out his mates just wouldn't see

So he taps again and washes his hands OCD 123

All That Matters

Count your blessings

The Judge on checkout 12 has secrets up his sleeve

If his colleagues had any idea they probably wouldn't believe

He's secretly into bondage with the judge almost anything goes

He's willing to give anything a try the thought of lust curls up his toes

He sits in judgement of others send them down at the drop of a h.

His ego is simply enormous I'm the bollocks and that is that

He looks down on everybody his chambers are his domain

He thinks he's well above the law it's all part of the game

He's totally addicted to sex any place anywhere anytime

He likes the feeling of danger and often steps over the line

He enjoys a kirb crawl around London the good time girls know him well

But one of them decided to stitch him up and she's taken the judg to hell

She sold him out to the tabloids his face was on every front page

They revealed his love of bondage he was seething with white ho rage

His sons completely disowned him he filled them with disgust

Glimpses of Life

He lost his job, which we all know brought in a tidy crust

His wife refused to talk to him his marriage of course is in tatters

The lesson for the judge? Look after 'All That Matters'

B & Q

You scratch my back and I'll scratch yours

The man on checkout 2 wonders why er indoors moans

He decorates people's houses but he never touches his own

She's been waiting 12 years for a kitchen hers is such a mess

She gets sick of his lame excuses saying which one today let m
guess?

His back is giving him so much pain he can barely stand up straight

She watches him on his way to the pub straightens up as he reache
the gate

The bathroom isn't much better it hasn't been touched for years

She's tried every trick in the book temper tantrums and tears

Her mate Elsie gave her a tip one day she said stop his conjug
rights

He'll soon get out his paintbrush dear tell him in bed tonight

He wasn't very amused he grunted that's a dirty trick

Next day he was queuing at B& Q muttering she gets right on m
wick

When she saw the tins of Dulux she couldn't believe her luck

Elsie fell about laughing and said there you go dear was it worth
F...?

Glimpses of Life

The kitchen was done in an instant the bathroom is halfway through

So ladies stop his conjugal rights and he'll be queuing 'At B & Q'

Don't Drink and Drive

A huge lesson

The male model on checkout 5 is wearing a worried frown

The court case is on Friday and he knows he'll be going down

3 times over the limit when he blew into the bag

A miracle they cut him out of his shiny e type jag

An entire family wiped right out if only God if only

His family have all been supportive but he feels so very lonely

The enormity of what he did will never go away

Why did he drink so much? Such an enormous price to pay
His mates had tried to warn him they begged him stay the night

He relives it all time and time again a horrific tragic sight

Kids toys were strewn across the road a doll and a teddy bear

He dreads seeing the family they'll think he just doesn't care

He'd give anything to turn the clock back have his chances ov
again

He detests himself and he truly regrets causing so much pain

He wonders if his life is worth living how can he ever survive

He should have thought of what could happen if you drink and the
you drive

Keep Your Mouth Shut About Viagra

Engage your brain before your mouth

The elderly man on checkout 1 needs to see his GP

The problems a little embarrassing but he can't get it up you see

He's fed up with making excuses headaches backache and more

His Wife thinks it's because she's put on some weight

And doesn't fancy her anymore

He keeps telling her it's not like that and he still finds her attractive

But she says if that's the case how comes he's not very active

Sometimes he hates her demands he's tried suggesting what they could do
How about joining a bowls club dear? She just laughs and says get you!!!!!

She keeps on about Viagra her mates hubbies a brand new man

She told her their at it night and day not exactly what he'd planned

He managed to get the pills then he decided to take 2 not 1

He kept her awake all night long she wished this had never begun

When she regained her strength she said I've been thinking about the Bowls Club

Perhaps it's not such a bad idea and there's always Darts at the Pub

But he had other idea's and said tonight I might even take 4

Put your fishnet stockings on dear don't be such a bore
Christ she thinks what next? Praps we'll hang from the chandelie

But it's far too late to change his mind she's tried to make thin
clear

The moral of this story? if you don't want your old man to shag y

Join the local bowls club and keep your mouth shut about Viagra

Obsessed With Your Looks

A boring pastime?

The young lady on checkout 5 is about to go under the knife

It costs her husband a fortune but he really loves his wife

She's about to have her 4th boob job but she'll never be satisfied

She says they miraculously get bigger everyone knows she lies

She's booked a tummy reduction a nip a tuck here and there

She's waiting to get her teeth capped and she's not happy with her hair

Her clothes are all designer her shoes? All made by hand

She's always first with the latest fashions and all year round she's tanned

The Surgeon tells her she's done enough she'll end with problems galore

But if she can only look even better she'll be happy for evermore

She's been flushed out countless times it's called Colonic-Irrigation

She loses weight every time so copes with the horrid sensation

She's had lots of liposuction she doesn't give a damn what it costs

As long as there's some reduction and her friends can see what she's lost

She's so into being slim yet she's built like a runner bean

If she puts a half a pound on she often lets out a scream

She's totally focused on her appearance spends a fortune on ne
beauty books

It's all terribly boringly boring to be so 'Obsessed With You
Looks'

Swinging

Not always such a good idea

The couple on checkout 9 are looking forwards to tonight

He finally convinced her, though she'd always put up a fight

It'll be good for our marriage it'll spice things up he said

We've been together for 9 years dear things have got a bit dead

The was totally against it called it the beginning of the end

Don't be so boring he said it's really all the trend

They logged on to the inter net trawled the various sites

They finally agreed on a couple and made arrangements for Friday night

They felt both nervous and excited as they knocked furtively on the door

10 minutes later it was all going on right there on the living room floor

The next day he felt really guilty she felt attracted to her new man

She booked a room at a seedy hotel but this wasn't part of the plan

After 6 months she was totally in love and prepared for many tears

He said what about us though? What about the last few years?

This was your idea she said I told you things

Would go wrong

Now you have to pay for your actions somehow you'll have to l
strong

The next thing he knew she was leaving setting up a new home

He sat on the sofa head in his hands feeling very much alone

No thought of their wedding day, and the church bells happi
ringing

Think hard before you make up your mind to try a little 'Swinging

Our Son

And so the book comes to an end and your watching us standing at the Checkout and so now it's your turn to people watch

The couple on checkout 4 have had their share of pain

They've cried tears to create a river time and time again

Their Son suffers from Schizophrenia there's been times that life has been hell

And like many other families they have horror stories to tell

Their Son has been to hell and back they both feel immensely proud

Their determined to help people understand which is why they shout so loud

There's very few cards or comforting words, compassion is thin on the ground

If only folk knew the strength it takes the courage that has to be found

5 years he spent in inpatient care many visitors? A handful a few

If he'd been suffering from Cancer they'd have formed an impressive queue

When he came back to live in the community he was faced with so much pain

By people who were his neighbours time and time again

They smashed the Security Lights the night he moved into his flat

They wrote letters to the local Gazzette we don't want nutters here and that's that!!!

They were judge and jury to our Son without even knowing his name
If they had insight into the past 20 years they would hang their heads in shame

The weight of being Carers rips many families apart

But they've managed to carry on with love for their Son from the heart

They both feel an ongoing grief for how their Son's life should be

There are times that they need some respite times they want to be free

The worst part for them is the stigma not many folk understand

So they try hard to educate people and dig their heads out of the sand

She's written books on their journey to be published in the New Year

In the hope that it might help others and helps dispel some of the fear
Respect is the least that sufferers deserve but there's still so much work to be done

Our inspiration has been provided by our own Beloved Son

www.ingramcontent.com/pod-product-compliance
Lightning Source LLC
Chambersburg PA
CBHW031209270326
41931CB00006B/478